Someday Somewhere Beautiful:
A West Coast Motherhood

Someday Somewhere Beautiful:
A West Coast Motherhood

Poetry by

Sophia Conway

© 2025 Sophia Conway. All rights reserved.
This material may not be reproduced in any form, published,
reprinted, recorded, performed, broadcast,
rewritten, or redistributed without
the explicit permission of Sophia Conway.
All such actions are strictly prohibited by law.

Cover design by Shay Culligan
Cover image by John James Audubon
Author photo by Elissa Landry

ISBN: 978-1-63980-706-2
Library of Congress Control Number: 2025932707

Kelsay Books
502 South 1040 East, A-119
American Fork, Utah 84003
Kelsaybooks.com

*to Christopher, my husband
who walks this path with me*

Acknowledgments

Thank you to the following publications, in which versions of these poems previously appeared:

The Hong Kong Review: "Sleepless"
Last Leaves Magazine: "By Willow Streams"
Love is Moving Magazine: "Dreams Like Yeats"
Sea to Sky Review: "Drowning in Sky"
Waves of Words Literary Magazine: "My Prayer Is Simple One"
Origami Poetry Press: "Crumbs & Constellations: A Haiku Story"

Contents

A Note from the Poet   15

Kindling   17
The Hymn I Sing   18
What I Didn't Say   19

i. Enda, My Child

Rapid Fire   23
The Bird Inside   24
the night blows   25
Abandonment   26
The Sound of Grief   27
Frida   28
Heart and Soul, I Promise You   30
Woman Hard as Shell   31
Sparrow Fly   32
The Study of Sparrow   33
What Is Yours to Promise?   34
Bouquet of Sadness   35
Nanoose Bay, April 2nd, 2022   37
The Absence of All   38
Fury   39
Imitation of Life   40
Runaways   41
The Ritual That Never Was   42
Two Stones   43
Losing Myself to the Grief   44
Dreams Like Yeats   45
Guard Your Heart   46
Seven Times I Missed You   47
For Souls That Soar   48
Our Genesis   49
Dedication   50

ii. Finian, My Son

The	53
The Weight of Life	55
Don't go to your sibling	56
My Harvest Song	57
Garden of the Soul	58
The Heart Is a Cavern	59
This Wild Place	60
Forever Yours	61
The Sun, My Son	62
The Reaper I Invited	63
Mother's Warning	64
Reflected	65
Ascension	66
Klimt's Mother and Child	67
Holy Ground	68
A Hurting World	69
My Song to You	70
Forgive Me	71
Born of Springtime	72
Your Mother	73
21 Days	74
Silence Your Critics	75
Give and Take	76
The Circle of Life	77
Your Cry Rises	81
A Slice of Constellations	82
In Dreams	83
A Journey of Letting Go	85

iii. To the woman I once was
    And the one I will become

June 9	89
My Tower in Babel	90
Everybody Wants to Be a Sunflower	91
Life's Gardener	92
The Weight of Things	93
What Does a Mother Look Like?	94
Between Worlds	95
My Prayer Is a Simple One	96
Foreboding	98
By Willow Streams	99
Drowning in Sky	100
One for the Night, Two for the Morning	101
Each Thin Strand of Gold	102
The Skylark's Song	103
From the Old Biscuit Tin	104
Rain Clouds	105
Sleepless	106
Rain Writer	107
206	108
Thirty	109
New Year, New Me?	
Unlikely	110
Brewing Hope	111
Healing the Whole of It	112
The Waters of Rebirth	113
Strength Like an Evergreen	114
The Artistic Bone	115
What Angelou Foretold	116
Mother Bear	117

Impact	119
Where the Geese Sing	120
A Death Like Autumn	121
Notes on Poems	123

A Note from the Poet

These poems are inspired by my journey to motherhood. The poems on grief and pregnancy loss may be triggering to those who have experienced the same or similar grief.

If this something you are still working through, I have shared some resources on my website that I have found to be helpful in my own grief journey.

For more, go to:
sophiaconway.ca

Kindling

He was kindling to a fire not yet fully extinguished but far from Joyous flame—gentle with his hands, kind eyes, drawing near. Not afraid to get burnt, no flicker of uncertainty at any ember or Sudden spark of mine. It bewildered me to see a man fall in love But saw a sincere heart in time.

Blue eyes and a smile that could light a room on fire. Brighter than me. Embraced in promises.

Who sent you here to me?
Who knew I needed you?

The Hymn I Sing

Your heart is a hymn to mine

An encompassing rhythm,
Spoken in reverence, reaching for
The divine.
Conspiring to make me majestic
Gossiping of something celestial

Hopes for many things but eyes
For you only, heart and soul no
Longer lonely. Together
We're a slither of heavenly thing

With you here
The wind does not cry
It sings.

What I Didn't Say

Your strength makes you beautiful
Stars wish they shined like you
Heaven marvels at your joy.
You are an evergreen in desert springs
Your laugh like bells ring among
The tallest mountain tops
And I wish to stand and stare
Forever and more.

Someday you will know
Your worth completely
May you then still find me worthy
This life to share for all eternity.

i.
Enda
My Child

Rapid Fire

More fear in this joy than I expected . . .
Thin blue line thin blue line
Two? One is too much but
Two could be perfect Two is
Joy unexpected and hoped for,
So much more fear than anticipated
And shock though we waited for
This moment for many nights now
Far behind.
Nine months and two blue lines means
Many million minutes where
This body is going to be
More crowded than ever before
Because it is not just I that
Occupies the space inside.

The Bird Inside

There is a little bird
Inside of me
Fearful and afraid
To stretch its wings and
Take up too much space.
Afraid to soar
For fear of falling,
Afraid to nest
If storms might come.

There is a little bird
Inside of me

A fearful one.

the night blows
over the brow of my
sleeping child

Abandonment

Motherhood abandoned me
Silently
When a beating heart became still
And a life slipped
From this rejoicing body
As a gentle spirit
Joined a higher choir.

Motherhood escaped from me
Suddenly
But I will find her
Once again.

The Sound of Grief

The power of words, they say, but
These tones fall flat and this mouth
Feels powerless.
Meditations into starless nights, words
Fill the silence but not the void.
Throwing all I know in to close the
Endless crevasse. Words like . . .

Love, peace, and beautiful things
Mercy, grace, and life-filled things
Hope and all of heavenly things

Psalms of lament, songs to a
God that allowed this
Plunged my soul into cold depths
Chords of words strung together
The only life vest. Now. Life.
Two shades darker

This
Lonely pace
This
Endless race

And still, my words rise into a
Sleeping dawn
And still the echos back and
No response

Eyes on this little sparrow too, please
Plans for a future and a hope too, please
Ravens to feed my soul too, please
If you truly love me too,
Please

Frida

The bus. burst into a thousand pieces . . . Something strange had happened. Frida [Kahlo] was totally nude. The collision had unfastened her clothes. Someone in the bus . . . a house painter, had been carrying a packet of powdered gold. This package broke, and the gold fell all over the bleeding body of Frida. I took off my coat and put it over her . . .
—Alex Gómez Arias (an eyewitness)

Our reflections overlap
I felt her shame
Here and now
And she my pain
And more
Long ago

Under the staring eyes
Of many around
And bright full moons
Of the bus headlights
Of the surgery room
Sweeping over
And eating into us.

Our nakedness laid bare
Never to be the same again
Hearts bruised by experience
All unravelled, all exposed
This hair is golden too

Broken bodies heal faster
Than broken hearts in this dark
They see every shy corner of us
As we soak the air with shame
Feeling polluted,
Desiring to be unknown again.

And grief
Like a tidal wave
Like a sweeping prelude
To what is still to come
And echo forevermore.

Our lovers in the wings as
We take center stage alone
And hope the audience
Can learn to move on from here
And not define us by our
Weakest moment
And this wretched truth

I wish to uproot.
Frida, Frida,
Do not leave me here alone.

Heart and Soul, I Promise You

This body did not nurture you fully

But this heart did not abandon you.

This womb cast you out in confusion

But this soul wanted you more than anything.

(I need you to know that)

Woman Hard as Shell

I felt pried open like an oyster
Knife slipping between rib and
Shell to dig into soft flesh and
Rob the pearl from me; one I had
Grown so tenderly.

Between bruised sheets later, I
Set my mind to grow another.
Strode my feet into the sand to
Find another grain and cup it
Between warm and determined hands
To nurture into something greater.

This one is mine.
This one they will never take from me.
Test me and you'll see.

Sparrow Fly

Savagely, they gave you to me in a yellow Tupperware box wrapped in a
Plastic bag stained with words like *hazardous*
And *biological waste.* I could have burnt the hospital down in my inner
Rage that they would place this great treasure in such a lowly space while
Realizing the grief that my arms had ached to hold you, but not like this.
Oh, I have never held plastic so tenderly. I held my own heart that day and
Wished the world would fall away. Our life a

Fable of how one can hope and
Love too much too soon.
Yellow box on the shelf next to the aloe until it was time to let go.

We named you in low murmurs that night
Enda. Our little bird had taken flight.

(With Irish origins, Enda derives from the Old Gaelic phrase Éan dála, meaning "like a bird" suggesting "freedom of spirit.")

The Study of Sparrow

Passer domesticus.
I wonder if we asked them what they
Wanted to be called or
Remembered and defined

A small, granivorous and insectivorous
Songbird. Large in character and
Widespread. But I guess they already
Know all that.

Appearance: Males—black bib,
Streaked-brown above and
Greyish-white underneath; Females—
Grey-buff everywhere. Only the males
Have crowned themselves.

Habitat: All over. They'll invade your
Pantry and, as with your mind, leave
Light crumbs of soft promises with a
Clutch of floating feathers. Find their nest
Within the ivy or under a thatched roof.

You will not notice them until they are gone
And wonder what was taken for granted.
They live for 3 years. You'll remember
Them forever. Their song in the early morning
Is the warning.

What Is Yours to Promise?

He pulls me close and fills my ear with
Whispers of faith, bravery and what is
Certain, for this moment at least.

All we need is each other.
At the end of the day . . .
I'm here, I'm here now.
It'll get easier, you'll see.

I have no words left to unpack
This blurred kaleidoscope of emotion
And have already glazed these floors
In tears. Waterfall dry, banquet
Ended, heart hollow. Your words
Echo but find no home within.

You care for me but can you
Put me back together again?

My grief is big.
Is your love bigger?

Bouquet of Sadness

Everyone brings flowers, not the type I
Expected for a death but pretty all
The same. The house
Is filled with them for weeks until they
Dry and shrivel out.
They are my only constant companion.
All others flee
When they see grief.

>   Lillys
> She murmured sorry at the door and
>   Asked if I was sleeping well.
>   *Not yet and probably,*
>   *Never again.*

Carnations
They were confused, I think, but the
Colors were pretty. Their tight squeeze
Made me feel whole again for a
Moment.
Wait, one more before you go.

>   A sunflower
>   I stand dumbfounded but accept the
>   Meal gladly.
>   Look for the sun. It's always dark
>   Before the dawn.
>   *Easy for you to talk about*
>   *Moving on.*

Petunias in soil.
Purple that matches my bathrobe. I
Wonder what you've been smoking
If you think I feel like gardening
Now. Later, I
Welcome the distraction.

                                                        Roses, all red
                        But passion got us into this mess.
                      I dry them out and make an old
                              Whiskey jar their home.
                          Nothing dies quite like a rose.
                    Suddenly I don't feel so alone.

The bouquet that is my home
Carpets the floor with fallen petals and I
Still find the odd one under the couch
And behind the shelves a year later.

The petunias bloomed last Spring.
One last blush for the two of us.

Nanoose Bay, April 2nd, 2022

Morning in the Bay
Slither of light			outward
Cry of a wild duck			outward
Hum of a waking world		outward
Grief flourishing			inward

Afternoon in the Bay
Gravel steeped in heat		outward
Excited chatter			outward
Shuffling of feet			outward
Grief shrivelling			inward

Evening in the Bay
Sunset hues			outward
Rush hour traffic			outward
Rustle of curtains			outward
Grief withered			inward

The Absence of All

So,
This is loneliness . . .
A thick blanket
Smothering slowly
Stretching over me
Bearing heavily down
As companionship flees.
Intentionality fading,
The silence awakening
As the seconds drag by.
What is life
Without you?
Eyes lift to empty corners
As I surrender to the silence.

Fury

I screamed so hard today
That all of life's joys slipped
And were ripped
Away
From my shaking body. I could not
Contain it all
But flung it at the four walls
That tried to imprison
This creature of fury I had become.
I swore I
Darkened the sun
For a minute until
The pain broke through
My heart
And my cry
Died a pitiful death.
I had no breath
Left to put anything into words
Emotions
Like a flurry of raging birds.
I felt powerful for a moment
Now weak
And hurting
Like a child
As regret washed over me
And forgiveness smiled.

Imitation of Life

Christopher
Should we bury it? Them? The baby . . . here in the garden, under a tree that we can plant. I've always wanted an arbutus.

Christiana
Let's not tie ourselves to one place. If we moved, my heart would always be here. Something like this tears you in half. Cremation is the way to go. Nothing left to keep us here, and they can go into a blue sky. Do the same to me someday. If you lose me, set yourself free.

Arbutus
Symbolises resilience and endurance due to its ability to grow in harsh coastal environments. They don't grow in a crowd. Winter storms do not break the human spirit, standing in one alone does. Borrow their strength but leave the rest.

Runaways

The grief weighs heavily, smothers
The air and laments in the wind

So we run
Pack the car with camping gear
And drive

To the ferryman, through Whistler,
Jasper, Banff, Calgary and beyond

Over mountains and between bare
Grain stalks we drive and sleep
Enshrined in colder nights and
Drink deeply of the winter sun

Sadness does not follow us but
The questions do. I hear them echo
In the mud behind each tire mark and curve

Why us . . .
Why now . . .
Why this . . .

On our return, we still have no answers
But a newfound peace, the kind that
Comes in waves promising
Something hazy in the morning light. I
Can't quite pin it yet but I can be patient.

The little white crib gets washed with
Tears and packed away

For a future day
Another hope
A different child.

The Ritual That Never Was

Healing was lost when I could not
Bury you, could not whisper my
Goodbye in your small ear
Comb a loose lock back
Into place, fold a blanket at your feet
Tuck you into your deep sleep.

The ritual of parting, the deeds of a
Final goodbye was out of reach.
There was no plot to bury you, no
Place to lay a rose for you, no
Ceremony held for you, no
Murmurs left for you.

I did not know you
I could not hold you
The ritual that never was
Was my last goodbye.

Two Stones

This stone slab I hold
Instead of your
Little warm body
Brings only confusion and pain
And I feel deceived
To have lost so much in you
And be left with what is cold and hard
Much like my heart these days.

Where are you?
Where are you?
Where are you, my child?
Come back to me.

Losing Myself to the Grief

Losing myself
Losing mysel
Losing myse
Losing mys
Losing my
Losing m
Losing
Losing
Losing

Dreams Like Yeats

I have spread my dreams, W.B. Yeats utters, tread softly.
Walk carefully, and guard each step ahead.

I utter the same words to this house, our home
Becomes a church shadow as each day turns over,
Light and day falling and rising around as I haunt
The threshold here.

The hopes and requests I murmur fuse with the old
Wood and new paint becoming one; a house of
Many dreams, and soon a life of many
Colours if I have my way.

I hear each desire whispered back in the stillness of the
Endless nights; echoes and mutterings, a flurry
Of prayers, clutching at meditations.

This home filled with wishes deeper than a wishing well.
My constant pleading becomes this shrine's endless bell.

Guard Your Heart

My ribs are close together
Like a row of tight needlework,
Like soldiers on guard
Afraid to let any emotion
To my heart.

A heart that needs to be hidden
And protected.
One that's broken too many
Times before.

Cage of white bone within
Do not let love through again.

Seven Times I Missed You

One
Post-surgery I felt empty. Have they really taken you away from me? They handed me a Tupperware box and told me three times not to look inside. *I Promise.* So much trust. Child mine. Child come. Stay with me another day.

Two
We stopped by a pizza place. I was starving. They asked me what I wanted. *Not sure. Anything.* These things were so important yesterday. Silliness. *God, they would have loved pizza.*

Three
The last time I saw what they told me was you, you were in the arms of the gentle funeral home man. *"Sorry for your loss,"* he said. I held no words that day. Declaration of Death. I never saw it coming. The paper in your father's handwriting hangs here still.

Four
Come one come all. See my shame. It's raining still.

Five
A birth announcement (not mine). I prayed for the earth to swallow me whole. I prayed for many things that day.

Six
October 3rd. We were supposed to meet this day, you and I.
I wondered where you are. Do you think of me?

Seven
This is the love I waited for; tiny hands, tiny feet, big heartbeat. We stand often by the ocean I wanted you to feel. I whisper in your brother's ear; *someday, somewhere, we four.*

For Souls That Soar

There's a fluttering in the sky
A meeting of souls, a growing
Glowing dawn
Clouds parting like a red sea
A shiver of wind, a quiver in the
Willow tree. There is a whisper
A bellow, a rumble, a cry
Singing being heard on high.

Stay sleeping, my darling
I am dreaming of you
Be humble, keep waiting
I'm coming soon.

Our Genesis

We shall meet in a garden someday
By swallows, by seashells, by sunset.

Beneath a vaulted sky of gold leaf
And washed apricots I will hold you.

Grief tried to take me but my
Victory cry to you will be *finally*

Finally.
I am here.

In the cool of an everlasting day
I will tell you everything

Every story, every song
Every thought. You

Will know the depths of my ocean and
I every star in your sky.

No tears, no fear, no goodbye
Just you and I

Where one declared
It is good *again.*

Dedication

To those   Entombed in lonely nights
Facing a colder dawn
With arms empty
Riddled with regret like bullet holes
Held together with good intentions
Waiting, waiting, for what?
With souls like a beaten nebula
Morphing into what is required
Empathizing with what is alienated
Unseen, unheard. Who are you again?
With eyes pinned on the horizon
Faced with the viper's saffron spit of disregard
Too far for second chances but still hopeful
Scattering thoughts, planting wildflowers of ideas
Honest only in dreams
In pain but continuing anyway
Conscious of the heavens spinning over them
Glass heart in hand

ii.
Finnian
My Son

The

Liar [noun] Synonyms: fabricator, exaggerator, falsifier, charlatan, distorter.
—Miriam-Webster Dictionary

Motherhood met me
In a fearful place,
In stunned silence
As the world watched on.

She took me by the hand
And told me to walk
Step by step
Ever onwards.

Day by day,
Her voice rang clear,
You are not the first
To walk this path.

Courage grows and
So will hope,
She urged
In starless nights.

Day by day.
"And then what?"
I asked
In desperation.

Life goes on,
She replied,
Alone or together,
It gets easier from here.

Children's laughter
Breaks the frozen trance
Of winter

The Weight of Life

I have carried many weights in life and you were not the hardest but heavy in a way I had never felt before.

The comforts were few and triggers many. You felt so much like the life we'd lost before your time which robbed us all of second joys and chances but still, we persisted. It was a slow trod every day, sometimes quick to the toilet bowl to throw up, faster to the pantry for a thousand moonlit snacks. You were my constant companion, always present but unseen, the cause of many things not fully understood.

The pain was sharp in my body but dull in our hearts as what-ifs swirled fiercely like the current that carried us through those endless days. I heard many women say how beautiful it felt and how they shined from within their wombs but I felt long withered as my body gave it all to sustain you. Each day the steps grew heavier and I grew rounder. Slowly we found our strength but were still impatient for the end.

At last, I birthed you next to the blooming sakura tree on an island between the sun and trees and we three finally felt complete.

Spiralling, rising—
Blossoms on a resurrected
Breeze

Don't go to your sibling
In heaven.
Stay with me.
Stay with me here.

My Harvest Song

He says that every once in a while
You have to give the tree
A harsh pruning for it to
Bear newer, sweeter fruit. This
Pruning for me is painful, cuts
Deep. What new life can this bear
For me? Hope dwindling, blood
Seeping, roots numbing. He says
Give it a winter; let grow the new seed.

Buds sprout, roots emerge,
And nests form within this tree.
Birds sing a new song above my leaves.
There is a blossoming in me.

Still in the silence, he mutters
Promises utters
That nothing comes free.
After the winter, I now see
There is new life in me.

Garden of the Soul

I weeded sorrow from my garden;
Grief from beds of roses.

I fought loss
And it pricked me

And I bled upon the bed
Of memories.

I ripped away the regret
That strangled my home

And burrowed deep into the dirt
To uproot shame,

To pluck out anger.
I watched as all my

Sorrows burned upon the
Fire into smokey dying skies.

A new year is coming,
I must start over

My garden fresh
For better days.

Sorrow has taken me
Too long, too much

Now joy and hope
Will flourish here.

The Heart Is a Cavern

He was given an Irish name
After me, my homeland, and my people
So far from here.
I return to Ireland at night. The
Rolling hills envelop me, the craggy
Coastline greets me, the
Wind calls to me. Its
Song is all around and inside as I am
A cavern that echoes back the
Melody from this foreign land. My
Son will someday meet this place and
Know his mother's heart
More deeply. I will
Teach him these words and
Listen to his heart sing too.

This Wild Place

It was slow and then quick.
I barely had time to wrap my
Head and heart around the
Realization as it dawned on
Me, not beautifully
But as messily
As this whole journey had
Been.

It's time
My body and the world
Around me cried. I heard it from
The clouds above—the
Sway of every perfect leaf
And each blade of grass beneath.
The sun was warm across my back
As if to wrap me in an embrace that
Could have been His. I found a seashell
On the beach, perfect and pure;
A gift from Him, I was sure
To remind me that I was not alone.

I couldn't stand the thought of going home
To stillness and cold surfaces so decided
To birth you here between sun and trees,
Wrapped in an ocean breeze.

This is a wild place, my child,
You will be wilder still.

Forever Yours

Your tiny hand
 Grasped my thumb,
  Our eyes met
   Across the years
    And I fell in love again,

Harder and deeper
 Than anything before.
  Never to be found
   In the depths of
    Your eyes brimming
     With tears

Or pried from
 Your tiny fingers
  That are now my shackles.
   My heart will never be far
    From you, my love.

I am forever
 Yours
  But you shall be
   A gift to many
    On the road ahead.

The Sun, My Son

My son saw his first sunrise today and
His eyes grew big as it
Dawned across the sea and hills and
On his beaming face.
Wide and crooked like your smile but
As beautiful as you were when
I first saw you too. You both
Fill my empty sky and warmth sinks
Upon my barren meadows, enticing
Growth, drawing strength from the
Ground; from it shall grow the
Strongest tree in me that will fill the
Sky with birds and dancing leaves
And flowers from the ground I shelter.

I saw the sun rise
In my son's eyes
Today
And pray that
This light shall never go away.

The Reaper I Invited

Motherhood is my body's enemy;
A flame that quickens through the
House that is my heart,
A thief that ravages the safe
That is my body.
It is the rust on the steel trap
Of my mind.
It calls to me in the deepest
Corners of my sleep and drags me
Awake at its tiny cry.
It demands everything—my
Strength, my patience, my marriage bed.
It is the ivy that, while beautiful, slowly
Suffocated the tree
Never to be set free.
It is the treasure
In the eye of the tiger that devours you
And the friend you invite to supper
That betrays you.

Motherhood
Heard my prayers for legacy
And she gave me
My desire; for this tomb
To be restored back
Into a womb
But
In return
For the first years of new life
She demanded everything.

Mother's Warning

Just you wait was the warning
From my mother to
Prepare me for the day
When my kids would punish me
As I did her when I was a child.
I lived in fear of having kids
Afraid of her words
Becoming a reality
As if she could speak
Worlds into existence,
As if she could see the future.
Deep in my heart knowing
That for my past wrongs
Enduring myself was what I deserved
Until the day in a new life
I had a son born from hope
For greater things
And love him I did
So much that it consumed me with a determination
That even if he became a past version of myself
I would endure it all
If only to share this life with him.
Time will tell if I am to be punished
Or set free of the past
And who I once was in it.

(I hope he takes after his father)

Reflected

I grew you in my garden,
Sheltering you from the heat
And feeding you what you need
So you can grow
And thrive. You soar
From our sacrifice
But are the mirror
That helps us see
The honest scales of our lives.
You live because of me
But teach me
To live again.

Ascension

I ascend to a gilded throne
Clutching the second life I've grown

Please . . .

This one is yours.

Don't tease. You promise?

Earth and sky, all mine.
But for now, yes child
I promise.

Klimt's Mother and Child

In Nevada
In the shower, I take you from your father
And you squirm until your little body
Touches my wet, warm skin and suddenly
You are home again in these arms, at
Peace against my heartbeat.

In Nevada,
I cradle you, red hair washes over you,
Eyes close to feel the heat and cascading
Water. Long eyelashes, pruned fingertips
And happy breaths.
This is us, the dream I waited to become
Klimt's Mother and Child,
With you, my son.

Holy Ground

Embraced and held
Tight as if I were to lose you
In a sudden storm this night.
Humming notes, finding the
Right start, higher, higher
Then lower again.
Your eyes lift to mine and
Droop like limp leaves in
Autumn; here but almost gone;
Old like the beams in this house
But weak as this withering sun.
Tones like a thread
Of fireflies ahead,
My song weaves you a path into
A deep slumber as we
Sway together into another night,

This ritual between mother and child . . .
Our sacred moment.

Your bedroom becomes our holy ground.

A Hurting World

Forgive me
For bringing you into this world;

It's broken
But I'll teach you how to fix it.

It's hurting
But you can help heal it.

My Song to You

Is
Broken and out of tune,
Raspy as the day I heard your first cry.
Eight weeks ago
You were first
Placed within these arms
That cannot hold the smallest song.
But to you
No angel choir can compete
With the voice
Of your mother.
She is like no other.
In your ear your devotion
Makes the crooked song
Flow straight again,
Bre   aks an earthly chain
And sets a melody f   r   e   e   .

Forgive Me

I wish you could see
You are the whole world to me
But forgive me
For gazing at the stars sometimes.

Born of Springtime

You were born at the same time as the world
After a long winter which felt much

Like the endless days of growing you.
As the daffodils emerged from the ground

So did your
Fingers curl their way outside the

Nurses swaddle. Few things would
Contain you both anymore.

I saw the sun rise in your eyes
For the first time and that smirk revived

Me too. You stretched
Like the saplings in the evergreen forests

High above. You and
The world outside my window bloomed

In all its glory, undeniable for all to see.
I saw hope in you and wondered what

You saw in me.
I knew this time would be short

And before long you both would move on
To older seasons but while here, I sit

And marvel at it all.

Your Mother

I live for your smile;
It lights the room on fire
And washes away the guilt,
Regret, and shame.
You give me a new name
And I am resurrected
To be yours again.

x Your Mother

21 Days

Finnian was 21 days old
when we loaded up the car and were
swept up in currents of the open road.

After all this waiting we needed to see
who we were now as a family of three.

White petals crowned the rolling waves
of Oregon, bristling pine trees painted
the skies of Washington, and golden
sands shifted and drifted across Utah.

In this foreign land, we felt free.
Furthest from expectation, ready to learn
to root ourselves together, feed you from
my body, sleep with you curled in the
crook of my arm, and love you even more
than I knew I could.

Me, greeting 29 on the edge of a
Grand Canyon. The one within now filled
by you.
Teaching you to be hungry for the world.
Hearts tired but eyes wide open.

In the night of a gravel lot by the railroad
your father asked me if I was ready.
For what?
This new life.
Ready and hungry like never before.

Silence Your Critics

My inner critic says
I write of love too often.
Ah, I say, but if you had felt it
You'd know it would take
A lifetime and more
To describe it.

Give and Take

There is healing in our children, an undoing
Redoing, a second chance
And several more thereafter.

There's a reliving, retelling, a legacy to
Impart, hope to build on, fear to invade
Newer promises to be made.

There are moments to create,
To take, to put to death before another
Generation, a cascade of better-mades.

There are knots that need to be tied the
Way my father taught me, and his before him.
Memories of laughter and shared moments.

Here is love to impart by the hands
Of all women before me, seasons and ages ago
They passed on wisdom so I too would know.

My life is just another stepping stone. All this
And more I want my children to know. Healing
Never comes too late.

The Circle of Life

I. Meeting

I saw 90 years in the 2 feet between the
Strong and limber bones of my infant son and
The endless shaking frame of his
Great-grandfather. You took each other in,
He with more consideration than you, my boy.

I couldn't tell if there was sadness or hope
Within his eyes to see his legacy arrive
As his days grew shorter all the time.
And what did you, my son, see in him?
Was it all the potential of life
Embodied here and now
Or the dying of hope that
No matter what you do, we
Still all end up here shaking and afraid?

II. Joining

Life in all its fullness showed itself
The moment your tiny hand reached
Across and curled around the withering
Bone of your great-grandfather.
Your eyes both met across the years and
I swear I saw an understanding there in
The brightness of yours and fading of his.

You will be him someday, as will I in my
Own way, and when the future visits as it did to him,
Our spirits will be gently lifted and we
Will feel hope again and then . . .
And then?
Hope for a long-earned rest.

III. Parting

Your great-grandfather passed away one
Storey down and two rooms to the right from
Where I laid you on the floor and
Played with you at night when
Jetlag kicked us out of bed and
Your cries tied us to the toys.

We didn't hear his last breath over
Your giggles and my yawns. We didn't
Feel his chest rise and fall for the
Last time over the softness of your
New skin and that hard wooden floor.

I wondered if it would have been better
For us to be asleep and we could
Have claimed ignorance that we missed
It all in our deep slumber
But instead, I wonder
If we should have sensed a shift in the
Air when the house was suddenly one less
Last night.

But maybe it was better this way. For
Him to pass in peaceful isolation, under
Soft cotton sheets to the apricot glow of the
Streetlight outside and the bubbling
Joy of his great-grandson above.

When life was slipping out of reach,
To be reminded
That a legacy hard-won
Continues in your son's son's son
And that while you greet your eternal sleep
The circle of life will keep spinning . . .
Keep spinning and spinning and spinning
Around.

Your Cry Rises

It's the first time I can't soothe you
And
Your cry shatters
The butterfly's wings
And topples heavenly beings
From their high places.
Your cry
It
Pierces the hardest heart
And I am overcome
With shame,
No, pain
That my love is not enough
To satisfy
And anger
That I was so naive
To believe
It could.

A Slice of Constellations

He kisses the cold glass again and again as if trying
To revive the winter dawn on the other side of the
Window. Days later the imprints are still there,
Intermingled with the buttery fingerprints that make up
This faded constellation.

I own this slice of heaven he makes just by
Being here, always near, my boy
Breathing, spinning, laughing without fear.

Jam smudges crust onto the window panes, its reflection
Is the ice forming like sugar crystals on glass rims
As the night falls. I scratch them all off
Before his father sees. These kisses,
These wishes of him
Who loves a big world from within.

In Dreams

Last night's dreams found me curled within a cocoon of
Tight blankets. In them was a straight road beneath arching trees;
Sunlight, warmth, meadows, even peace maybe?
I pushed an empty stroller within a bubbling crowd of small
Children whose faces blurred when I looked closely. They parted
Like the Red Sea when my Granda walked towards me.
I've lost my son. Help me find him, Granda.
An old familiar smile, a wink of the eye, his round face
Full of new joy and old life.
Again as when he was alive, I could not understand the
Thread of words he chuckled out as he brushed on by
Drawing the children after him all in a line.
I turned to follow them just as they blurred into shifting colours
Before a growing light. Beside me, suddenly my son filled the
Old white stroller giggling gleefully.
The country road ahead stretched endlessly.

Star-shaped crackers—
My son's mouth now full of
Crumbling constellations

A Journey of Letting Go

Fresh into this world
You are completely mine
For now
But slowly and daily you will become
More and more your own and then the worlds,
Straying farther and farther from my arms
Inch by inch and then in miles
As you spread your arms wide
And take it all in
As you should,
As you're supposed to.
But I will always be here
Kneeling where I first held you,
Single tears and silent heartache
With arms empty
Watching your every move
And always worrying more than you.
Waiting, waiting
For you.

Grow big and fly my child,
Higher than all before you
But come back to me
Someday
Somewhere
Beautiful.

iii.
To the woman I once was
And the one I will become

June 9

My mother would swear I was born to rebel, fill
The air with stubborn thoughts and flood my
Boots with anger. I was a small rage, barely
Tall enough to hang off the schoolyard fence
But still, my furious legs tried to launch me
Over and flee into a world of words and books.
The year and the day behind prophesied my divisive
Drive, second-guessing and proud mind.

On this day in 53, Nero found life in a new wife but
15 years later would lose both to his suicide. What
More can we say . . . Love and life, both gone this day?

Leo Vincent brothers take a life for Al Capone in
1930, 94 die in '53 Massachusets, a coup in Bulgaria
In '23, *have you no sense of decency, sir* hears Joseph
McCarthy in '54. Secretariat wins, and so does NATO
And Yugoslavian peace. My parents too for that matter
For on this day I landed in their arms and took my
First breath. 1995. A winning year, a mother's pride.

This one day, almost holy to me,
But somehow less sacred than
February 18 and March 23.

My Tower in Babel

I once wanted to be an architect and
Crumb by crumb, place myself
Into the sky
Reaching heaven, eyes skimming the
Feet of holy ones
Build myself a road upward, each storey
A level closer and
Once complete, breathe a clearer air
Before leaping down to earth, murmuring
Of bright stars and
Sweeter music, falling like a
Stricken angel to the soil below to
Remind us why we cry
For higher things. Dust myself off, pick up
a brick and begin again.

Even after all these years, many utterings in
Foreign tongues later, we have not learned
Our lesson, we still yearn for heaven.

Everybody Wants to Be a Sunflower

Not every flower is courted
By bees and butterflies.
Some live quietly
By the roadside
And bloom
Only for themselves
And the sun to see.

Life's Gardener

for Hannah McMaster

After the three heartbreaks my mother, a gardener, took me to her orchard and beds of flowers beneath the outstretched arms of trees to teach me how to garden too. I didn't see the point of it amidst my great heartbreak until she explained that I must learn to recognize the weeds in the flower beds and in life too; those who sprout quickly with empty promises and deceiving beauty whose arms offerings are bare. Weeds: only a parasite.

Volcanic crater—

Do not be deceived by the strength and pain of briars and thistles; they will always be fearful but their roots are shallow and uproot them we can all but they'll try to stop us from believing we can. Briars and thistles . . . so much to gain if you do not let them stand in your way.

Roses are beautiful but bloom too quickly and leave with nothing; dependent on the care of others, never standing on their own but cling to stronger bones. Don't be a rose, grow an iron spine and do not give it all for one who blooms so briefly.

Below, the bud that blooms

Sunflowers are here for the sunny days and bright rays but do not ask them to stick to your side and guard your back on a dark night. Sunflowers can't be found when life gets hard. They are no friend of ours.

Marvel at the daisies, my dear; humble and persistent. Yearn to be like the lavenders who grow in drought and are hardy against the winter storms; their strength is small but they are gentle and welcomed by all.

Unafraid

The Weight of Things

My weigh scales were broken for a while
From the many heavy things
It was forced to hold, cups battered and
Bruised, losing sight of the
True value of things.
Years it took to fix them again
To weigh the world and everything said
Carelessly before
See what was true against shiny things and
Fools gold
To remind myself what it was all for.

I hold things tenderly now, less
Recklessly
With a pinch of salt, with knowing eyes
I look at it all, judge carefully
But let less inside.

What Does a Mother Look Like?

I watch myself
Pack my beautiful clothes into black plastic
To be dropped at the door of another
To wear and love much better.
The feeling of pride
That I could let go and bless another,
That I could make myself lighter
By the renewing of my wardrobe. *Minimalism*
What a beautiful word
That I could be worthy of
Such modernity
And follow the surging crowd around.
I'm a mother now, I must dress like one!—*Aha!*
The truth simmers in layers of
New words, temporary trends, and feel-good thoughts.
I do not have to change because I am a mother.
This is to be my evolution!
For my son,
For my husband,
For me,
But can you now see
It's to justify an identity lost. I look different now.
Plain clothes, loose layers, nothing shiny here.
When did you grow up?
Why so sensible? (What a horrible word!)
The mirror does not lie. I do not see myself anymore.
Are you still there deep inside?
Too ashamed to put up the missing person posters of myself
I hide.
Where are you . . .   Sophia?

Between Worlds

I went out to feed the cat last night.
That tabby who haunts this
Place more than I do
And saw the moon hang
Before the veiled darkness of
Night and the way it lit
That old country road alight
Like a river of solid mercury.
I swore the wind called to me
And the bare branches of
Frost struck trees beckoned
Me as they swayed.

I wanted to go down
That old familiar road that was
Transformed this winter night to take
Me somewhere new entirely,
To leave this world behind.
A body ready to run back to freedom,
Back to young adulthood with all
Recklessness and joy.

My heart
Though hooked by a dimly lit room
Within that held my curled-up son
Who had entered his deep rest under my
Watchful eye.

I wanted to be there for him
More than anything

But also to feel light again
More than everything.

My Prayer Is a Simple One

I threw myself upon Mount Sinai[1]
And demanded answers for my shame.
This pain
That burns within me is often stronger than
The peace I know exists[2]. I want to
Know what it is to feel truly free, to be
Burdened with love while weightless in fear[3].
I want you to answer me
From the storm around[4]
In a whisper as I cover
My face too,
For my soul to be fed by ravens in a desert[5]
Place where hope has died. To fly with[6]
Eagle wings and outrun the world with[7]
Strength only of you.
I don't want to understand. Keep
Your revelation[8]
Such knowledge is too glorious
For me. My shoulders are too small for
Glory. But
Give me a pure heart and show me[9]
Your face

---

[1] Nehemiah 9:13
[2] John 14:27
[3] Matthew 11:28
[44] 1 Kings 19:13
[5] 1 Kings 17:2-6
[6] Isaiah 40:31
[7] 1 Kings 18:46
[8] Daniel 2:21–22
[9] Matthew 5:8

So that I can find the courage to
Finish this race[10]
And hear you say,
"Well done."[11]

---

[10] 2 Timothy 4:7
[11] Matthew 25:23

Foreboding

I try to take it all in
But it's hard. It goes fast
This life, these minutes.
Clear like crystal but suddenly
Muddy and far across the horizon.
In every moment a foreboding that
All good things come and then come to
Pass. I miss all of them, these little moments
That are my children almost; treasured
And unique, born to me and loved
Deep. Here and gone too soon
Like my son, like the son of
Yesterday. Here and gone,
Here and gone so soon.

By Willow Streams

This fruit tree does not grow that tall,
It is not laden with many fruits, sweet
And ripe, ready for the picking. It does
Not want to be picked at all but left in
A quiet corner of the orchard covered
With many blankets of white blossoms
And courted by the humble ones with
Their stripped armour of gold. It has
Short and knobbly branches, not here
For you to climb on, not here for you
To prune. It sits by the Willow stream
And has worked hard to find its peace.

Move along, gardener.

It is not here for you at all.

Drowning in Sky

It is silent in the house when
The fog seals it from
Across the lake where it gathered
Its might and prepared to
Ambush us at dawn. Only the
Hum of the old refrigerator dares
Break the stillness of being cut
Off from the world.

I switched off all the lights to
Feel fully what this bright darkness is
And how I can become one with it. The
Stew on the stove boiled unlike the
Rippling stillness of the cloud around and
I wondered if they would ever find me again.

In moments, I hoped not but only to escape
Into this new peace I had found in my
Cottage now hidden on top of the world for
All to know and none to find save for those
Who dare wade into this deep gray ocean.

I shall be happy here; unbothered by the world
And untempered by its storms.

I will live quietly   here
I shall live peacefully   here

here
Drowning in sky.

One for the Night, Two for the Morning

The unwavering but not unwelcoming floor
Under fluorescent lights that beam a
Cone around me and shelter me from
The sleep-soaked whimpers of my
Son next door and his father who snores
Less softly.

This book is my anchor to another land
That welcomes my escape after a
Long and hard day being Mom, being
Wife, being Me. I've worked to escape
From all three, here
On the bathroom floor in silence.

I shall soon curl over the last crisp
Page and have to lift anchor, adrift
Once more in my reality navigating
The uncertain waters here and the
Possible mutiny in
My marriage bed, in the high chair of
My son, the voice inside my head.

Water hot and wet threatens
To bubble over the metal edge before
I pour my cup and watch it simmer
Happily down into the tea bag.

One cup of red tea tonight
To leave this world behind
And two of darkest coffee
In the morning to give me strength
To take it all on again.

Each Thin Strand of Gold

Postpartum hair loss hit me
Long ago and continues each
Day and every shower where
My hairbrush is overcome with
Thin strands of gold and the
Shower walls are left displaying
The contemporary story of
What it is to have had a baby.

I comb them out, each lost strand;
Every one of them represents a
Part of me now lost to motherhood.

I love him
I love him,
I love him, my boy,
But I miss me too.

The Skylark's Song

A skylark perched upon my window
And I saw its song knit my soul
Together again . . .
Less beautiful than before but
Swimming in melody.

From the Old Biscuit Tin

I ate the last biscuit,
I felt entitled to.
After all
I birthed you
And that was hard.
●

Nine months of heavy labour
Before labour even began.
Five hours in total.
They tell me I was lucky
But five hours is still
Five hours in pain.
◕

It rained
On your father's cheek
When you landed on my chest
For the first time . . .
You've lived there ever since.
◑

Now I guard you at night
And sustain your life
Hour by hour
Minute by minute
Available for your every need
And whim and cry
And that is why . . .
◔

I'll eat all the biscuits I want.
I'm a mother now.
The body that bore you
Deserves it.
○

Rain Clouds

Psalm 51:10

Rain clouds gather
Over my meadows.
I welcome it.
Wash me clean, I cry,
Cleanse my soul.

Sleepless

I am well acquainted with the lonely hours
And the shadows that occupy the world at night,
Especially those in the darkest corners of my house
That makes me question the light.

I know the ~~silence~~ of night well,
The stillness that hangs between the sheets
Only allowing the tip tap of rain through
And my heartbeat LOUD within my chest.

I know the s h a t t e r i n g of nightly rest,
The craters underneath my eyes
And yawns which are my body's cry
For a world of dreamless sleep
Yet unreached.

I know the streets outside my window,
Transformed into much unknown,
The shade of every dim streetlight below
And how they stretch and grow.

I know of tiny lights around
Not normally found
When day breaks across the skies
And thesetwoworldscollide.

Rain Writer

I wait for the rain
And then I write.
I can't do it in silence
When I feel under my skin
The silence of the world weighs as if
It's waiting with bated breath
Throwing me in the spotlight, urging me

WRITE
GO ON
SPEAK

I can only write when it rains,
When the heavens are storming
And the ground is pounding and
The air gasps aloud.
Only then is it safe for my words
To slip out. In the moment when no
One hears a pin drop in the rage around.
When all eyes are turned upward. When
Noise and movement are all there are, I
Look inward and speak,
The words trickle slowly but true.

One for me
And one for you.

206

Mine was the first body my mother
Made. Weaved in darkness, threads like
Firelight in warm depths; knitting bone,
Embroidering fingerprints, eyes like buttons
Eyes like my father. A body whole
Until I was stolen into bright cold
Daylight and God exhaled into me.
Captures by dreams, enamoured with
Heaven, gasping for life.
Out of the forge and into the fire
Ready to sing, to fight, to run and fall
In love and puddles, waiting to
Dance in this kitchen with you
Thirty years later, weak arms that
Now carry a son, a body that made
Another body. I was her first and he is mine.
A legacy of life, a calling to hope,
The reminder of what love can create.

206 bones within . . .
One for every hope
I carry.

Thirty

I'm almost 30 and keep finding
Pieces of myself the world over
Shards behind of a life abandoned and
Crumbs ahead of a future self one prays
For but is too afraid to hope for.
Burning to be a second sun they marvel
At and not its lost reflection.
The weight of curiosity, desires
To know who I am to be
This late but better now than never
Burrows deep and strains the threads
That patchwork my life.

Still here, still me
Wondering, praying, seeking
The world over but, with each new day,
Finding me
Still me.

New Year, New Me?
Unlikely

This year will be different,
I whisper
As I pack my bag with tears and fears
Of the past year
To bring with me.

This year I'll be a better version of myself,
I murmur,
As I put on the cloak
Of my old self and fill the pockets
With doubt.

This year it will all come together,
I say,
As I pass by the new road and
Take the one walked many times
Before.

Maybe next year,
I sigh,
As I made my old bed
With a heart afraid to change
And a head full of lies.

Brewing Hope

He said *meditation through action* on the TV screen
And an email earlier that day asked me what routine
I could make into a ritual to unburden me
To grant my life more meaning, to set the anxiety free.
I chose to make coffee
As I always do but this time with great intent, as if it
Held higher meaning, as if this is what I was born to do.
I ground the beans and let the water brew
Symbols of pain for a greater gain, bringing each
Bean to the end of themselves.
Water hot. Love burns too sometimes.
I stewed the two together, counting seconds, the
rotations of the spoon.
Adding milk to lighten the bitterness. Hope and purity?
The clinking of mugs. Bubbles rising. Release
The hard things.
Steam winding. Are these my prayers rising?
Now it's just me and my cup. No answers, just
Questions flood the kitchen.
Not sure if I thought hard enough
Or if I'm overthinking this.

Healing the Whole of It

I felt as though my body could
Heal. Yours at least as I pulled you

To myself and held you
Fiercly. I urged kindness to surge through

Me and into you, strength through the
Arms that hold yours, compassion

Head to head, and forgiveness hot
And cold between toes.

Particles of skin, each
And every hair, hot breath between

The mountains and valleys we are
Together in this moment. Hardness of skull

And softness of palms open to give
And receive freely, murmuring, *Please.*

I imagined opening my eyes after and
Seeing you fully healed, complete

Like ever before; glowing and
Rising in strength.

Disappointment found me between
Wet lashes and though you felt still

Broken you had been whole for a
Moment, now and someday soon again.

The Waters of Rebirth

I made a bath
With milk and honey,
Of Turkish delight
And everything nice
So I could sweeten the bitterness
Within me and drown the lemon tree
That grows ripe and sour within my chest.
I swore to never rest until . . . until?
Until I could be sweet again
And greet the morning dawn as innocent
And loving.
The new me will be better still
Than all the old me's left behind.

Strength Like an Evergreen

Wide but not tall, brimming
With bristles, surrounded by
Trees all in a line.
Evergreens
Teaching us resilience,
Not to falter in any season,
To be bold in the winter when
All others die.

You were not the biggest
Or most beautiful. You were
Simply mine once I laid
Eyes on you and maybe you
Thought you had been deceived
By my look of affection when the
Axe first hit your trunk,
Leaving only a stump.
How wrong you were for
We took the best of you and
Lovingly dressed you up to be
The centrepiece
Of our home.

Draped in gold and silver and light
You are still small
But now
The most beautiful of all.

The Artistic Bone

The artistic
Bone in my body
Is gathering dust and rust
From abandonment
But tired
From days it was
Pushed too far
And almost snapped
But it yearns
For talent untapped.

The artistic
Bone in my body
Is a neglected reminder
Of my unfulfilled potential
So I bury it deep
Not wanting to keep
This reminder of
What I could become
If I tried harder.

The artistic
Bone in my body
Waits for the day
I pull out my pen and paper
And start to write away.
It reminisces for days of old
And hopes for days of glory.
This artistic bone of mine
Isn't finished with its story.

What Angelou Foretold

See me, the lotus,
Rising out of the mire
That is grief, the sludge
Of lonely nights, the
Deep waters of doubt.
Now swollen with hope,
Bathing in a cleaner air,
Soaking in joy.

See me rise, Maya,
See me reborn.
This creature of might,
It is I.

Mother Bear

1

Mother Bear came to comfort the infant on the night his mother had had too much wine, cooked out on the couch, shame for few to see. The baby's cries rang clear and high but only that great lumbering shape came to comfort him. She had lost her cubs earlier in the Springtime and her heart hurt to mother another. She was gentle, I'm sure, and my son must have laughed at her twitchy nose and round ears as he does when he sees the pigs in the yard. She must have thought I'd never know but who leaves paw prints in the nursery? Not I.

2

Mother Bear came again when he was five and ten. Both times he cried as he was pushed to the tarmac, black as she is too, by older boys whose stories no one believes about a roaring demon who chased them away, standing protectively over the whimpering shape of the boy nursing his knee. *Liar, liar, little boys* but she didn't know I saw her too as I rounded the corner.

3

Mother Bear had better instincts than I did. He realized such encounters were not normal the night he lay broken on the highway out of town. She lumbered her great body over his shattered motorbike and lay over him. It was a cold night in October and he would not have survived it otherwise. They didn't believe him either that time but I knew he spoke the truth and thanked God for her life.

4

Mother Bear was curious. He saw her for the last time in the back garden when he had two girls of his own. The two stared at each other for almost an eternity before his daughter's terrified screams drove her away. It was they who told me of the great black monster that visited that day.

5

Mother Bear felt it. I spotted her silhouette on the edge of the graveyard's tree line with her cubs, finally a mother again when I was not. There were no sounds, only knowing eyes that day.

6

Mother Bear is a good hunter but I still leave pork sausages out when the winter is hard and food in the forest for the young bears is scarce. By morning there is nothing but large pawprints in the mud. Some say they see a family of bears in the graveyard every Spring smearing honey on headstones, and others speak of a great black beast with shadows longer than night.

I tell them all that I don't believe such things.

Impact

My world collided like a comet
But twice as unlikely and half as
Satisfying when, in Paris,
While struggling with my stroller
I caught sight of them . . .
Twirling, laughing, feather light
Before the Eiffel Tower steps.
I saw myself in them
Five years ago next month
And wondered what became of me
And what I did become.

Tonight I crouch in a half-lit apartment.
My companion's loneliness and dissatisfaction
Along with the sounds of my baby snoring
And the space my husband takes.

I wonder where they are now
In Paris, in love
In a bright room filled with warmth
And laughter.
I wonder what became of me
And what I did become.

Where the Geese Sing

Where the grass meets the ocean is
Where we made our home.
Built it strong on blankets of
Autumn leaves and snow.
I drank deep the ocean breeze and
So did my son's lung
Gulp it in
When his life had first begun.
He was lulled to sleep
By a chorus of
The frogs and woken by the
Song of the geese.

When they flew south for the winter
I didn't have the heart to tell them
That we wouldn't be there in the Spring.
They will still call this home and raise
Their young by the wetland but we
Are now made for another place.

A Death Like Autumn

My death comes slowly unlike Autumn.
Fifty years of growing older while
The earth here dies in three months.

White hair, curls like creeping ivy.
The golden dresses of maple far more beautiful
Than these robes worn by many before me.
Bark hardened by past winters. These hands
Have seen many winters too. Neither of us chose
Where to be planted as saplings but I've moved
Further along.

Empty nests. Empty arms. We were both
Homes to many that are now long gone. My back grows
Bent while yours grows tall. The tallest trees are
The oldest, they say. I only counted a tree's rings
Once. I hope they don't count my wrinkles ever.

I heard butterflies live for 2 weeks and bees live
As long as 60 days. How terribly short, I always thought,
But now I know that Methuselah thinks sadly of
Me too in her $4,853^{rd}$ year. What is my 86
Years to her? This great intelligent species
Outlived by a pine tree in California.

Will you remember me, Methuselah, when I am
Soon gone and resting three layers beneath the
Sun? Will you
Remember my death, far less beautiful than that
Of the earth this Autumn? What stories will you
Whisper to the birds about me next Spring? Wrap
Your roots around me as I sleep so that I
Will not rest an eternity alone.

Notes on Poems

Kindling, The Hymn I Sing, What I Didn't Say: Initially, I was only going to focus on my journey to motherhood with myself and our two children in mind, but very quickly, I was confronted with the reality that this journey wouldn't have been possible without my husband, Christopher. And so the book begins with three poems as acknowledgments to him (any more than that, and he would have been too embarrassed). I owe him a lot; he loved and supported me through this wild journey so far, and I dedicate this book to him with all my love and gratitude. Our marriage isn't a perfect thing (as hinted at in later poems) but there's no one else I'd rather do it with than him.

Frida: I'm fascinated by Frida Kahlo's art and her life story. My surgery experience during miscarriage reminded me of the feelings of vulnerability and shame she probably also felt.

The Sound of Grief: "Eye on this sparrow" from Matthew 10:31. "Plans for a future and a hope" from Jeremiah 29:11. "Ravens to feed my soul" from 1 Kings 17:6.

Nanoose Bay, April 2nd, 2022: Learning to carry grief well takes a long time. In this poem, the world is moving through the day in its busyness but grief is a slower march and an inward journey.

For Souls That Soul, Our Genesis: These two poems are both a yearning and celebration. As much as I enjoy our son and try to be present with him, I am also aware that heaven holds another little treasure for us and we eagerly await that day when our family will be fully reunited there.

The Liar, The Reaper I Invited: These two poems are harsh and speak to my disillusionment with motherhood in the midst of grieving a miscarriage and struggling through a second pregnancy that was full of emotional triggers. I love being a mother but felt it was only honest to acknowledge the hard moments of this life-changing role and the sacrifice it requires.

The Heart is a Cavern: As an immigrant, it's challenging for me to raise my son in a culture I did not grow up in and still have lots to learn about. There are days I dream about bringing my son back to Ireland where I grew up and teaching him about the places and people there. I feel that until he can fully experience my own home culture, there are many things he will not be able to fully understand about me.

Mother's Warning: In my mother's defence, I was not an easy child. *June 9* speaks to this too.

Ascension: After experiencing the loss of a child you often feel like you're walking on eggshells after. Even after having my son, Finnian, there are moments I pray to God and ask if I can have him a little while longer, or check his breathing in the night. There are some losses you simply can't move on from. This poem is one of those moments where I imagined asking God for more time with my son.

Klimt's Mother and Child: This one is my favorite artwork of Gustav Klimt! As a redhead, I see myself in this painting cradling my son. It's one of those intimate moments I live for as a mother.

iii. Poems: These poems touch on many themes, including self-confidence, courage, transformation, dreams, hope, and the tension between humility and the desire to become something greater. Looking back on my life I'm amazed at who I used to be and all the hundreds and thousands of tiny choices and detours that have brought me to where I am today. But this journey isn't over yet and who I am now isn't who I'm meant to be forever. I believe in God's transformational work in my life until the very end. Motherhood has brought about many of those transformations and moments of growth.

Healing the Whole of It: Speaks to many moments of prayer shared with my husband.

Mother Bear: A short story of mothers looking out for each other, the inner bear our children release in us, and the tensions of it all.

About This Mother

Sophia Conway is an Irish poet and writer residing on Vancouver Island on the West Coast of Canada. She can often be found writing poetry, eating cinnamon buns with her husband, or walking the beach with her son. Much of her inspiration comes from her Christian faith, her search for belonging as an immigrant, and her motherhood.

Learn more at:
sophiaconway.ca

Soli Deo Gloria

www.ingramcontent.com/pod-product-compliance
Lightning Source LLC
Chambersburg PA
CBHW060838190426
43197CB00040B/2677